T0368218

Mental Roads

Mental Roads

Art Dohrmann

Library of Congress Control Number:		2024908552
ISBN:	Softcover	979-8-3694-2076-8
	eBook	979-8-3694-2075-1

Print information available on the last page.

Rev. date: 04/25/2024

To order additional copies of this book, contact:
Xlibris
844-714-8691
www.Xlibris.com
Orders@Xlibris.com
854191

CONTENTS

Camping Roads

2:16 AM March 27, 2023. For some reason I woke up thinking of when Wendi had gone to Gov.'s school. Apparently she and her group had broken the code which limited the amount of time they could communicate with each other after Gov. school. I remember talking to a moderator of the communication system was extremely frustrated that the system was always busy. They didn't understand how this could happen I was secretly proud but didn't tell that the students had broken the code. James from Minot showed up again and again in our lives after we've moved from Richardton Taylor. Jen had attended Gov. school before but no indication of rules being bent I have looked several times for the fossilized sharks teeth that Wendi brought back from Gov. school excavation.

The summer after my junior year in high school I attended a 4H conservation camp at Lake Medicago she. I was amazed that everyone knew that Stark County was a bad place. The previous year the girls who attended the camp had been expelled for breaking curfew. We know nothing about this. It was a wonderful place to mix and mingle and maybe learn something. I learned that I had ignored 47 mosquito bites on my left arm because I was too busy learning something else the night before. Wendi also attended an international music camp at Lake metigshoe. Dave and I traveled up to Lake medical she to pick her up after the camp. Donna, Jen and I spent 10 days in Scotland and London as we had bought tickets to a event that was canceled. Donna was charmed by an uncle who kept calling her Lassie. The major downside of that travel was jet Jen became sullen. She was missing Brian. I have encouraged my daughters that I doesn't hurt to kiss a few frogs. If the frogs don't turn into a prince at least a frogs feel like a prince for a while. Donna and I were parents of two beautiful girls. I don't know what Donna told them I simply stated keep your brains above your waist.

Our family enjoyed camping it was an inexpensive way to spend time together. We started with a pop-up tent. On one such trip in South Dakota it turned cold and we ended up with all four of us in the sleeping bag that Donna and I had that we could zip to together we woke up with for in the in the sleeping bag. I remember the walk we took the next day there were wild raspberries were right we had a cup that we picked the raspberries into at least some that we didn't eat and that evening we bought ice cream and had fresh raspberries on the ice cream. We next bought the pickup camper. Several times during the summer the Taylor Rod and gun club which I was a member of would camp out at Lake Sakawa. We would pull the boat out camp for a couple a days and go fishing when the weather was nice. Traveling was fun in that pickup and camper except when we looked in the mirror and Jen had printed on paper or stop stop stop we pulled over and stopped and found out that there was a spider in the in the camper that they wanted me to kill. We then bought new two way radios that would we could talk to one another and not rely on pounding on the window which we didn't hear or put in a piece of paper that we might be able to read. We took the pickup camper to Minnesota got Kirsten and Karen Hemg to come along and we were going to camp out at Bemidji we had a route planned the second night out it rained and rained and rained and Donna and I were sleeping in the tent away from the pickup but we had a moat of water between us and the pickup camper we found out they were scheduled to rained for two more days so we packed up and spent that time in a motel. The pickup trailer was sold and was replaced by a stock rack for the pickup and I used cattle trailer that I borrowed from Dennis washed out and moved necessary belongings to St. Paul. It was more than 10 years later when we were living in New England that I bought another camper. This was a fifth wheel camper that we could pull the boat behind. Many Sunday afternoons Donna and I would take the camper Lake Sakaweah. We would arrive at campsites just about the time most people were leaving so we had a very quiet Sunday evening and most of Monday to just sit and enjoy. One Sunday afternoon we drove to visit Bill and Leon Wagner who were staying at the cross ranch on the Missouri River. We ended up staying with them for two nights. We ended up spending several nights with the Wagner's both in North Dakota and also to a cabin they had in Wyoming. Bill Wagner was a high school friend of mine and the pastor who spoke at Donna's ordination ceremony. I still remember the gist of the sermon each day the sermon is to deliver meat and potatoes to sustain the people for the week or the month or the year until they returned. Eventually we gave the camper to Jen and Brian to use, they used it to buy their first fifth wheel camper.

Summer fishing trips were important part of dad's family gatherings. On two different occasions we want up to Lake of the Woods and rented a cabin and went out fishing for two or three days in hired launches. One morning Dennis steps off the dock fell into the lake between the dock and the boat I remember dad dropping to his stomach pulling this wet kid out of the water. Fishing that day was delayed while dad and Dennis went to dry down change cloths and go out fishing again. After grandpa died dad and Clarence and Willie family went up into Canada on number of times to fish I not one time I was running a boat I was probably freshman in high school or eighth grade I don't remember Willie Severson. Kenny and Sherman were in the boat. Fred ran a boat that Clarence and someone else were in and dad had his own boat we fish along the shore and were about a mile from the dock when suddenly the wind came up this little wooden boat had 18 inch sides and seats for people to sit on when the wind came up the waves were 2 1/2 to 3 feet tall I had no idea if we would make it across the lake. We all have our life vests on and I told everyone to sit on the floor of the boat Willie moved further back to the boat to sit down but then the boat was so unbalanced I had to ask him and everyone else to move forward in the boat until it was level. The wind came at an angle to the direction I needed to go so I would have to angle into the waves and at the crest of a wave I would turn 90° and then follow the waves it took at least four or five turns trying to time the turn at the top of the wave so that we did not capsize. I remember this event not whether we caught a lot of fish are not.

One summer Ron and Lucy and Larry Marcusen and myself and I don't remember who else went up into Canada nor the Regina. We launched on one lake and maneuvered through a channel to another lake to where we were fishing this lake was perhaps 2 miles across or more, once again we are on the far side and fog came in and we had not I had not a clue which way to go. Ron was running the boat and he said I think we go this way for 20 min. or so we cross the lake in a fog and when we approached the other sure we were very close to the channel to get to the lake to where we had camped. We had two tents Ron and Lucy were in one tent and the three guys were in the other tent. On the way back near Regina the water pump on Ron's car gave out and the car overheated. We left Lucy in the car and we walked down to the stream about a half-mile away to collect water to put in the radiator and attempt to get to Regina. When they got back to guys had stopped to help this poor girl alone in a car, they seemed quite disappointed when we walked up out and carry water to put in the radiator. They helped us into Regina and found a place where we can get the car repaired as we were discussing things they had gone to Lake Sachawea that weekend and the two of them had caught a lot more fish than we did up in Canada. As we approach the border we had a few more fillets and we could legally bring into the United States and Larry was absolutely frantic about it I told her when we get to the border laydown close your eyes and pretend your sleep don't say anything don't do anything. After we got to the United States Larry sat up of right and just white with fear that we would be arrested for bringing too many fish into the United States. This was the last time we went fishing into Canada for many years.

A critical trip was taken in my eighth grade summer. Two adults seven children of fully pack trunk and on our new 58 Buick and a car top carrier were heaped full. I had a temporary drivers permit so I practiced driving on the way up and back. The normal seating was dad, and mom in the front row one kid in front and the rest arranged in the backseat every 50 miles we would stop and rotate a position. When I drove mom sat in my position and after 50 miles or hundred miles she would come to the front and I would sit where I was supposed to be in the rotation. As we aproched the motel in the Regina where mom and my sisters stayed for the four days the odometer turned to the 50 mile mark and a clamor of voices we pulled over and everybody moved positions to begin the next 50 mile segment even if we were less than two blocks from the hotel. Priscilla and Erna were small enough to sleep in the back window where they spent most of their time unless they had their front seat rotation. We attempted to tell the story for mom and dad's 50th wedding anniversary. Everybody wrote up a little bit of their memories. At this time I concluded that we were all in the same car but we're in different universes. By the time we return my permit had expired and I had not taken a drivers test. Dad called Selle Ward, a ND highway patrolman told him about the trip. Dad was asked if I was a good driver he said yes and a week later my license arrived in the mail. A drivers license is a mixed blessing. I could go where I wanted but I also had to take family and cousins to events that I wanted to attend alone. A number of times when my date would be sitting beside me and I drove home to drop off my brothers and sisters and anyone who did not have a date after league. Luther Leauge a joint meeting between the UCC and the Lutheran Church. Clarence and Bernice Haugen were the adult sponsors of the event the highlight of course was the Easter Monday banquet. This was an opportunity to take your best friend out in public. My sophomore year in high school I was asked to do Junior senior prom by a girl I scarcely knew. I felt obligated to invite her to be my date for Easter Monday. Two evenings with this girl were enough.

One of the fun games was called the wink them the girls or the boys sat on chairs with one person standing music would play and what you would walk and when the music stopped to try to find a chair whoever was left standing was eliminated and one chair was removed. Somebody would attempt to wink at someone across the circle as they got up the music started again and the elimination continued. One evening Clarence was going to give a demonstration on how to kiss a girl. He handed Bernice Haugen two glasses of water told until her to hold them shoulder height and then he approached to kiss unfortunately he got two glasses of water dumped on him. This social event did not exist for our children.

After league most everyone would go home. One evening my date had to be at home right away. As a return to Taylor I saw lights in the church. I went in and talked to the girl whose brother was on an date. She lived about 25 miles from Taylor south of Richardton a area that I had never been. Much later her brother found us near the house and the to return home together. Donna could never quite understand this casual interplay of friends when we were in high school. We had vastly different opinions of what qualified as a date. Done apparently never had a group of friends in high school. Donna had a troubled childhood. She was a baby of the family for seven years and then became a forgotten middle child. I don't recall her talking about any interaction with her older sister. She described the evening meal often featuring the dreaded tuna casserole. Homework feeding the fish and playing solitaire appeared to be her major distractions.

Years later after our children were in bed we would talk about Donna's frustration about never having learned to be a mother. Donna joined a group of mothers (La Leche League) who nurse their children for at least six months of their life. Here is where she saw and experienced mother and child relationships.

Disparate Roads

For breakfast I had half a waffle with strawberries and whipped cream. I visited many intriguing places on this tour but they all resonate like one hand clapping. My life is divided into phases. Alone before I met Donna, the wonderful world shared with Donna and our girls and now.

One of dad's pet peeves was when we would pick up tools and moved them or anything else wander off and leave them somewhere else. Dad made the comment that the next thing that we left in the wrong spot he would spank us with. I believe this was called the hand of learning applied to the seat of knowledge. Dad had fixed an old steel wheeled dump rake that is sitting in front of the shop in preparation for use. I started climbing on the steel wheels which caused the rake to travel to the middle of the yard. We had a huge pile of used lumber in this area just known as the dump pile. When dad returned home he told me that was too big for him to spank me with what I needed to put it back where it belonged.

About this time dad's high school friend Rudolph Stoxen came to visit. Dad, Rudolph and Elmer Jurgens had in high school best friends. Rudolph began to reminisce about high school and after events. Dad stopped him cold and said it was time for the kids to go to bed. I got into my pajamas crept down the stairs to and avoided the squeaky steps, crawled under the kitchen table open the door to the basement went to the basement and out in front of the open window where dad and Rudy were talking. After hearing a couple of stories I was cold and tired so I returned to bed and fell asleep. Some time later I pulled the prank that dad thoroughly disapproved of. I believe I put some gasoline and an old pressure cooker that had been discarded a placed the pressure cooker in the shop behind the car and threw a lit match into it. Poof!!! The flames shot up to the roof and I was fascinated by all the spiderwebs that were burned. Dad was not fascinated as he contemplated a suitable consequence for me I asked the question. What had happened when he was bringing a brand-new combine from Richardton to the farmstead. According to Rudy story dad was so drunk on the way back he drove into the ditch at least twice. Dads comment as he walked away was that Rudy tended to exaggerate. Another story I heard at that time was that dad and Clarence would hide their liquor in the culvert between where we lived and where they grew up. However grandpa Fred discovered that site and they had to find a different spot. Another story I heard was when the three of them were coming back from a party in Lefor. Someone was taking a leak on the hood of the old model A Ford. The urine stream splashsd on the spark plug and the spark followed to hit the poor individual in a most sensitive area. Dad also told about when he was going to school in Wahpeton he was dating a girl there and also dating a girl and Taylor who worked in the post office. Apparently the girl from Wahpeton sent a postcard to dad which his girlfriend and Taylor read and sent on in an envelope The Knights of Columbus club in Lefor was the site of many social events. Bachelor parties, bachelorette parties, wedding receptions and regular steak fries were all held there. A common phrase was that people caught the Lefor flu. I believe Jen mentioned smelling some really funny smelling tobacco at event held there.

An important fall event when I was growing up and when our children were little was soup and strudel. This was primarily a Catholic tradition the soup was made from beets and onions and carrots most everything from the garden and whatever meat or sausage they had available. I remember seeing a 30 gallon pot in a farmyard heated with wood and prepare to three days before the event. Soup was always better the second or the third day. The strudel was made from a pastry dough rolled and filled with various condiments. My favorite was Apple, then pumpkin but I also remember cream of wheat, cottage cheese and another vegetable filling whose name I don't recall. We attended these almost every weekend for much of the fall. These events were held in Lefor, Gladstone St. Mary's in Richardton the Catholic Church south of Richardton, New Hadrack, Killdeer, Halladay and Dodge. By the time this season ended we were ready for Thanksgiving. As the years passed and the women who did the work could no longer do it this tradition died. St. Mary's in Richardton would take orders for strudel for several years but is not what I remembered.

One Saturday morning I'm looking at the old 1961 GMC truck that dad bought when I was a freshman in high school. We went to Dickinson to pick it up dad told me I could drive it home. I was so proud to be the first person in our family to drive it. It was only a cab and chassis one who got it home we put the box and hoist that had been on the old Reo truck on the new one. My first solo drive was in the old Rio truck. We were about a mile and a half north of the farmstead and dad had me drive the truck home. I was too short to reach the gas pedal or the clutch or the brakes so dad put the truck in the first gear (double gumbo) then turn the key push the button to start the truck and steer, at home when I get into the yard he said just turn off the key and I did. Another drive with the old Reo Naomi had a drivers license so she drove the truck to the elevator in Taylor. We unloaded the truck but as we were leaving Naomi scraped the side of the elevator with the truck box. Apparently I was older then so I backed the truck away from the side of the elevator and drove out the door to the street. Then Naomi had to drive because I didn't have a license yet.

Both trucks were used for grain harvest. I was supposed to bring the truck to the combine when dad waved but I occasionally I was asleep at the wheel. I remember listening to music on my new 8 transistor radio. Another time I took a mare south of Taylor to be bred. On the way back I met a combine going down the road I didn't even slow down I just drove on and wondered about the look of terror on the people's face. I then remembered I had the stock rack if I had been closer I would of broken off the combine auger and probably broken the stock rack. Dad owned this truck for many years. Dad then sold to Russell who used it for grain truck and had a bale rack built to fit on it. I bought the truck from Russell shortly before he died and he eventually sold.

For several years Dennis rented the farmland by Lefor from Elmer Diers. One early June when helping Dennis finish up seeding there I saw seven tornado clouds but none came to the ground. One evening driving back with Dennis his old pickup lightning struck a telephone pole beside the road and parts of the pole hit the windshield of the pickup and into the open passenger door window. The best was when Dennis, Russell and I would take two trucks down to pick up bales. One would drive one would load the bales off the ground with a pitchfork and one would stack the bales "idiot cubes". We rotated position for each truck load. Usually the last load of the day would require a stop in Gladstone for a few beers.

My first farm truck with the 1973 Ford I bought at auction sale in Minnesota. I paid $600 for the truck and stored it at Gene Redlin's place north of Fargo until I could drive it to the farmstead. When I fill the gas tank in Fargo the price of gas was 20.9 cents per gallon. But because I bought more than 40 gallons I got a four cent per gallon discount. At the time I knew I would never buy gas that cheap again. I believe the current tax per gallon of the gasoline is over $.18. I also bought a red Dodge pickup in Fargo. This next spring after school ended I was going to bring back all the supplies for myself, Priscilla and Joeset. We had more than I could load in the pickup so I had Fred bring a towbar from his farmstead and I bought an old car that did not run at a auction. When I picked up the car it had a flat tire so I swapped with the car next to it got things work together and headed west. It started to rain before it got to New Salem so I pulled into a service station. I asked if we could store the pickup in the station overnight. They said yes but we could not be in. We unhooked the car drove the pickup in the shop and made room in the car for us to sleep the night. By 6 AM the rain had stopped we moved the pickup out and hooked things back together and then on our way west.

Another spring I was heading to Taylor with my Plymouth car and pulling a motorcycle on a traitor. I stopped at a rest area and a trucker with a flatbed pulled in and came over to talk to me. He said when I pass him there was a terrible rattle somewhere. We loaded the car and trailer onto his flatbed And he drove me to the farm. I believe I paid him $20 for the ride and found out that is only loose lug nuts on the trailer that cause the rattle. This was the first time I saw the little white pills that keep your eyes open wide.

Father's Day 2012 I'm on my way to pick up Gavin. What a wonderful Father's Day gift. As I enter the left turn lane I remember the first time I had ever seen a left turn lane. I didn't know why it was as a junior in high school I was driving in downtown Minneapolis I wondered why that Lane was always open so I would go into the lane and then signal to get back in and drive on and on I finally realized what I was doing and thanks heavens for North Dakota license plate which was a kind of get out of mistake free card.

Flashback to Vietnam. Early one morning my company was taken by truck to a village that we had never seen before. As I got off the truck and officer in the Jeep came by pointed to me and to others and told me get in we have a place we need to fill. We set up for the day and the cemetery outside the village that was being swept for contraband. We were told no one was to be allowed to leave the village. About an hour later several kids came running toward the cemetery. As they approached, we shouted "Didde Mau" which means leave fast. They kept coming until somebody fired some shots into the ground and front of them and they ran away. All day we heard explosions. I counted 29 helicopters coming in to pick up wounded. I heard the officer that picked me up had been wounded when his Jeep hit a mine and one of the people in the Jeep was killed. I don't remember how I got back with my company but as we left we had to walk in the tracks that a tank had made because the ground was so mined you didn't dare step anywhere else. This story was confirmed by Tony Baxter 40 years after the event. Several weeks later I saw elephant tracks beside the trail in the jungle. I found out we had been in Cambodia on the Ho Chi Minh Trail. At this time I developed a raging staff infection in my right leg. I believe this is when I contracted malaria. When the company went back less than a week later I stayed at firebase Libby because Roberto Salazar refused to let me go out again. At this time Roberto, Robert Cook, Sgt. Cox and four other members of my squad were killed. Three months later and 40 pounds lighter I return from Cam Ranh Bay hospital. I spent two days with the squad of whom I only recognized two. When they got to the brigade main base(BMB) I tested for clerk typist and had two different job offers. Nothing like a little stress to improve your typing skills. We had work detail every day at the BMB. One of the detail leaders asked if anyone had construction experience. He was leaving the country in three days and needed somebody as a replacement. I took over this position and was personally assigned to a command Sgt. Maj. Floyd Smith. He told me to do what ever I was asked to do and he never wanted to see me again. I saw him again when an acquaintance of mine was being court-martialed. He asked me how I was involved in the action and I told him I lived in the same building and was walking by and called to be a witness. The staff Sgt. who initiated the action got a little payback. First Sgt. Scheffy asked me to write up reenlistment interviews for everyone in the company. I saw the staff sergeants record and entered a report that he not be considered eligible for reenlistment. I don't know if this had any effect on his future. The answer my friend is blowing in the wind.

Giving Roads

Donna was a most giving person I have ever known. The second time I talked to Donna she said she didn't have time to talk to me. And walked away. I followed her and asked what she was doing that was so busy and so important now. She finally related that her roommates had talked to her that morning. They accused her of trying to steal me from Nola. I said I had called Nola that night only because I had met her father in Bucytus several weeks before at a Democratic function and I didn't know anyone else at D S U. she finally believed me but said she would talk to Nola before we could speak again. Donna finally admitted she had a wonderful time the first night we met, but did not want to get in the way of anyone else's relationships. We spent some time with her drama club friends. I soon asked her why she was always willing to go fetch a beer, cleanup of mess, set the table or do whatever else was asked of members of the club. She said that's just who she was.

A few years later on New Year's Eve were in the bar of Gladstone. At the stroke of midnight, we kissed and everyone was screaming and shouting and kissing except for one individual at the bar. Donna walked over and gave him a kiss. From what I knew about Denny E I don't believe he had ever been kissed before.

One evening as we were window shopping at the Nicolette Mall we stopped at a shoe store. A rather tattered looking man was standing at the window looking at a pair of shoes. Donna found out that he had a job interview the next day he had clothes but what he wanted nice shoes. We talk him into the store and bought him a new pair of shoes. When we left the store Donna said not to buy her a Christmas gift because that was her gift. Money was tight for us Donna received $1000 a year for books and tuition from a donor in the Red River valley. I had spent much of the month before I came to visit working on a cash flow projection for the Farm credit system and the farmers home administration. The plan was approved but Judean Brousseau said there had to be more. I told him about the gift to the seminary in Donna's behalf. The following year I worked with a Farm credit counselor. I submitted my numbers and he changed him to look better. I signed the proposal and it was approved. I had arranged to sell the farmstead and 160 acres to LJ and Janet Dohrmann. But it took an additional $10,000 loan from dad to pay off the divorce from the Farm credit system. Judean asked about my experience with the Farm credit counselor. I told him I didn't mind lying to others but refuse to lie to myself. I told him the proposal that had been approved was the biggest pack of lies I ever signed my name to. I told him the sale of the farmstead was pending and everything would be paid off within a month. I wrote a letter stating I would push a rope up the Missouri River from Bismarck to Williston before I would ever borrow from Farm credit system again.

March 31, 2023 at 5 AM I lament that the invention of the electric light. A clear call warm morning, the sky is full of stars. I walked all the upper decks of the ship and nowhere was there not bright light to block the view of the stars. On every ship I've been on I've asked why they do not have a place to see the dark sky. I remember the first night I took Donna to a dark place. We stopped on the road by the old Haugen place. I believe we had recliners we set him up and layed "to put or place" down and just look at the stars. But soon we saw other lights it was a firefly night. I told Donna this is where I went to drop all the cares of the day, the year, and in the world. An hour or so later Donna just whispered thank you this is when we shared a neutral nourishing place better than sleep we could relax and renew.

I heard the same stories from at least three individuals. They were shopping and looking and enjoying what was offered for sale. Later Donna would give them one of the things ahead especially enjoyed. They said they had to tell Donna not to buy anything for them. I on the other hand have my life flooded with mementos of Donna. The sandals I wear every day possible, the yoga mat where I tried to do my daily exercises. The bicycle I ride in Bismarck is rolling on tires she bought for me. These physical gifts I never turn down I said thank you with a kiss and a pat on the butt. We are a couple miles off the west coast of Mexico I told an acquaintance I would swim to shore and walked naked to North Dakota if I could experience that touch again. More than 100 times this month while transcribing this I need to stop and cry.

When Jen and Brian were ready to buy their own RV trailer Donna say just use the one we owned and they used our trailer as a trade-in. I I believe the car Jen was driving when she got married had been one we gave her. We got the old car she was driving to the dealership they looked at it and we were going to make a deal when I got out I told them don't turn the car off the battery is so bad it won't start again. Among the things Jen took to set up her first house in Sioux Falls was a microwave. They wanted the microwave but not necessarily all the stuff I put in the microwave that I thought they should have. Donna rolled her eyes and shook her head when I told her what I had done but admitted she had added some things into their items they took to set up their house.

When Donna performs funerals the funeral home normally gave an honorarium to the pastor. This was taxable as other income but in many instances Donna returned this honorarium for their family Memorial. She also gave an unexpected gift to the owners of price funeral home and East Gates funeral home. She told the owners a limerick. Did you ever think, when a hearse goes by, that you may be the next to die. The worms crawl in, the worms crawl out, the worms for pinochle on your snout. Apparently none of these owners had ever heard this before. She laughed often when shared feedback about this limerick.

In our first year traveling together in the motorhome we had driven to a restaurant for supper. The meal was fantastic and huge we were not prepared for southern portions. We carried two large to go boxes. As we exited the restaurant two individuals were their asking for food the next thing they knew they had two boxes of food and were told it's still hot if you want to eat it now. When the churches we visited I believe in St. Charles Mississippi had put together zip lock bags with items for homeless people. Donna soon created quite a number of our own packages to give out. A bottle of water several energy bars and hand wipes were the things I can remember. I believe we soon included a five dollar bill.

Sometime after we were married we were talking with Florence and Carol and then Donna started talking about living and working in Bismarck. Donna said one day as she was leaving class in the sixth grade another teacher smiled at her and said a pretty girl like you should have a great day. Florence said she remembered her girl from another class that had seen one day, and described the clothes she was wearing. Donna said that was her in her favorite outfit and having the first smile in a week after that greeting. One never knows when a good deed will come back to bless you.

One of the most fun things we did was to get our sons-in-law to sing. As we travel Donna and the girls would break out into song mostly about movies. Usually the just fun little songs, but I remember the first time that Jen and Brian were riding with us and everyone was singing and even Brian joined in. I don't believe I have ever heard him sing after that but it was fun at the time. When we traveled with Wendi and Daven singing spontaneously occurs. We have heard Daven sing much more regularly in the last couple of years. Ari has a choice of which parent will sing him a song before he goes to sleep. Donna would sing a song but one parent got the last song.

The aspect of giving support that seemed to bother Donna most when a person attempted to get her to support one point of view in order to counter discussion. Donna had a class on triangleation, where people try to get the pastor on their side. Donna was willing to let discussion flow. I heard from a council member who said many decisions were delayed when Donna suggested prayer and a return to the issue later. This method seemed to work as several of the prior council chairs had left the church. My way or the highway was not useful to strengthen a church.

Donna was not exactly one to seek adventure, as she had enough just moving through eight or more houses before she left for college.

Moving to Dickinson was the first time she gone west even to Mandan. Donna was always ready to give it a shot. When I met Donna she had several more unsatisfying experiences behind her. Donna shattered the ice around my heart! She sent me into a tornado of emotion so when she said she loved me I was so shocked I did not know how to respond. I saw a phrase recently "she is sunshine with a bit of hurricane" The first winter and early spring we spent as much time together as possible mostly between classes or after she got off work at 10PM. I had found her class schedule which helped. Russel had crops near Halliday and Dennis had crops near Lefor plus our crops and cattle near Taylor. Over 70 miles from north to south, Russ was still in the army, Dennis was in training for the National Guard and Dad and Mom went to Alaska. I gave Donna a green VW Karmen Gia I had gotten from Pris. Donna had never driven a stick shift before so she practiced on an old pickup started to drive the VW from Bismarck to visit me. Donna's mom called the VW "the poor little thing".

Donna learned to drive a tractor both to help seed and to pull stuck vehicles. Then came trucks, three wheel and 4 wheel atv's, snowmobiles and to ride horses. She taught school, directed school plays, worked in a book store and became the manager of a Christian book store. All this while being a lover, wife, and mother! Donna joined an ELCA program called Associates in Ministry which lead her to become a Pastor. Donna has arrived at her role in life. She could learn, lead, teach and nurture in a calling she had heard since sixth grade. Our family life changed from living on a farm to St. Paul Mn. at seminary, Bismarck for internship, St. Paul and on to New England for Donna's first Call. Seven years later Donna accepted a Call to Bismarck where she served until she retired. Jen, Wendi and I followed as best we could. I joked that as soon as our daughters graduated from high school we moved so they didn't have a place to come home to. We traveled as much as we could, twice to Mexico, twice to Europe, once to Italy. We followed the east coast from Boston to the Florida keys, we followed the Ohio river to the Mississippi down to New Orleens. We traveled central U S to Texas and Arizona west to California and north to Oregon and always home by Colorado to see Wendi. We flew to Portland and Seattle to cruise to Alaska and visit family and friends. Our first travel outside the US was to Winnipeg for our honeymoon. We visited Hawaii with Loren and Lois Myran. Donna was always amazed that for someone with little expectation of travel we sure got to go a lot of places. We tired or RV travel and bought a house in Texas for winters. Donna died before we could live in the Texas house. In the last two and half years I have cruised around South America and visited Egypt. The original transcription was done on the cruise around South America and now edited at South Padre island Texas March 2024.

Long and Winding Road

The cousins club was an important part of the social community of Taylor. It seemed like everyone was related. The Dohrmanns, Marcusens, Stoxens, Myrans, Conradsons, Haugens, Seversons, and others. At one such gathering when I was dating Donna everyone got a name tag showing their generation relationships, Matilida Stoxen (Tillie the Toiler) made a special tag for Donna that read friend of the family. Many years later when Wendi was seven or so there was another gathering. When they came to me and asked a question. Why is Annie fifth-generation and I am fourth-generation were the same age. I told them they are part of the family that married late. Dad was 30 years old when he got married. And I was 27 years old when I got married.

Dad had mentioned many times that he had pursued Edna Diers for seven years before they got married. A story he told about when he was 20 I always find him very amusing. Grandpa Fred and grandma Caroline took Florence and Carol to the Chicago world's fair in 1930. Somewhere around the house we still have some moment those of that trip. Before grandpa left on the trip he had written down the mileage of dad's car. When he returned he found out in that time. Dad had driven his many miles as grandpa had driving to Chicago and back. Dad never complained but only commented on the Sundays I would drive into the farmyard in the late afternoon filled the tank with gas again and be gone. One of dad's high school graduation gifts was a custom-made Miles city saddle. Dad talked about going to get fitted for the saddle. Then they made the trip to choose the leather and the hull that he wanted. Dad also regularly attended the county fair and Ekalaka Montana. Dad Clarence and Willie also attended school in Wahpeton after graduating from high school. Among the pictures I have seen was the three of them with their arms around Indian girls. Dad never talked about this but he always said always look at the mother before you fall in love with the girl. The first time I saw Donna's mother she had just finished a shower and was wrapped in a towel. My take away memory is now I know how Donna got such great legs. One afternoon after mom and dad were married as they were driving home mom said pull over to the side of the road. There in the road ditch were some yellow wild roses. Mom wanted some of these to transplant at the farmstead. I have tried numerous times to transplant some of these flowers into take into Bismarck with no success. The flower still bloom every spring.

Life is a dance you learn as you go. Sometimes you lead, sometimes you follow. Now I just wander. The first Facebook I composed after September 22 was the day the music died. I miss being led. I posted the picture bird trapped in wire fluttering, flying, and slowly dying. I guess I'm in need of rescue.

2011 was a wet year in western North Dakota. There is extraordinary snow cover over the entire area west of us on the Missouri River drainage. The Corps of Engineers is projecting flooding just from the snow melt. And then it rained and rained and rained. Lake Setauket we are was filling fast. The river had Bismarck was 3 feet over flood stage. This had not occurred since the 1950s. Dikes were built and houses were lost. A family from church was in danger of losing their house. I offer them the upstairs portion of the duplex we owned in Mandan. The renters had left with no forwarding address and ruin carpets throughout the upper portion. All the carpets were removed and replaced. The couple with the three girls who rented from us did all the work in lieu of rent. We cleared everything out of the our basement in the house and Bismarck. Even the new carpet we had just put down I cut out and piled on chairs. I cut a hole in the basement floor to put a sump pump in case we got water in the house. We had sandbags around most of the house a pump in the sump hole a standby generator in the garage which fortunately we never had to use. The river crested at 5 feet over flood level and maintain that level for several months. Downriver from Bismarck a Levy had been breached and 135,000 acres of land was flooded. Everything from the basement was loaded on a 36 foot flatbed and stored at Al Sankey's Place until we could move it back. The recliners and chairs did not come back. Cats had slept on them and Donna declared them junk.

At the farmyard Taylor things are also very bad. About 20% of the farmland was too wet to plant. To get to some fields I drove an extra 10 miles. By the June 10 cutoff date for crop insurance I quit seeding. Only parts of the fields had been sprayed before seeding. I got there a twenty foot air seeder stuck where it stayed for almost 6 months. The fields were full of weeds but only some of them could be sprayed again. The air seeder was a half-mile from the farmstead my 100 foot sprayer ended up a mile and a half from the farmstead. We collected insurance for prevented planting. Which was better than a kick in the head. Harvest time was more of the same. The combines at and the trucks required long drives to get to where I wanted to go. I loaded the trucks less than half-full and tried three different routes to get to the grain bins. I had my tractor parked near where I always got stuck pull the truck to a dry spot and didn't the same thing again with the next truckload. 10 years later those ruts are still visible. Cindy's brother Rodney is renting Cindy's land. I don't believe he's gotten a full crop in the eight or 10 years he has been operating it. Many of the fields are permanently ruined by excess water. The snow in 2023 was heavy which is now bodes bad things for that area again. It depresses me to see so many acres of land not producing.

Time stamp. March 1, 2024

Feb 27 2023 I flew to Rio to begin a cruise around South America and write the memories Donna and I had recorded. From Rio we flew to Iquaza Falls for a wonderful time. We flew to Bonus Aries began the cruise arriving April 6. Dennis called on my birthday perhaps only the third time in my life he called. He said that the ALS was much worse and 75 and done! May 7 was a benefit for Dennis which all his family attended. July 5 Jen, Gavin, Wendi, Ari and I met in Cincinnati for some family tine at Diane's home. In late July I began radiation treatment. Sept 14 I met Wendi's family at West Yellowstone. Nov 20

I flew to Egypt for 12 days. Dec 14 I was in Arizona to meet Naomi and on to Texas. Dec 24 I flew back to Bismarck to try to see Dennis alive one last time. Dec 29 Dennis died and I had seen him one hour. The funeral was Jan 8 and on Jan 10 I flew to Colorado to visit Wendi on my way to Texas. I am attempting to edit what I wrote while I am in South Padre.

Rhodes Scholar

When I got to the Isle of Rhodes in 1970 I did not see a trace of what was known as the Colossus of Rhodes. One of the seven wonders of ancient world was completely gone. Too much of my past is gone.

In a conversation with Tony Baxter we discussed the affects and effects of Agent Orange. The affects of the chemical were to kill all plants by disrupting photosynthesis. The effects of men in contact with this chemical was prostate cancer and death. This effect was not recognized by the Department of Defense and until after a vast number of Navy personnel who handled the chemical had died. I can remember walking through jungle where nothing was alive. From the 50 foot trees to the smallest sliver of forest growth nothing was green.

Soon after I left the company to go to the hospital Tony talked of one night they had very close contact with the "NVA" North Vietnamese Army. Tony and Hudson had dug a foxhole which was rarely done. Hudson was killed by friendly fire, a helicopter gunship fired a fraction of a second too early. I asked Tony if Hudson was a very tall attractive Negro and he said yes. That said Rock Hudson had been my assistant gunner for almost 2 months but before I left he changed. He was no longer excited about going back to Chicago and becoming a pimp all he could talk about was his mama and the past. This was one of three instances I knew about where people quit looking forward and only to the past and live for only a few days before they were dead. One person committed suicide self-inflicted another ran into enemy fire and was killed and Rock Hudson. Another incident we talked about was when the company set up a night defensive position "NDP" ambush squads were sent out about 300 yards. If they made contact they were supposed to call in and we join the company position. One night the sergeant leading an ambush got scared and pulled back to within 100 yards of the NDP. About 4 AM one of the people on the ambush lit a cigarette and Joe Simon a soldier from the Solomon Islands and whom I really liked opened fire with his machine gun. Brown was hit in the leg and got his million-dollar wound. A million-dollar wound was when you were not killed but injured so badly you are not returned to Vietnam. Tony said he had no pictures from Vietnam so I showed him mine and he is selected about a dozen to take to Staples and have enlarged. The enlarged photos showed a lot more detail than the little pictures I had taken with my and somatic camera.

After Tony left the infantry, he got a job driving truck. Not a nice safe job but often to go out and pick up the remains of helicopters crashed trucks that had been burned or ambushed. Tony talked about another friend he lost and said the man's name and I said I knew him and I had a picture of the truck. This individual was the first I had known in a long time. I don't remember the name now but I got to know him because he got out of the infantry had a truck driving job and had just gotten married in Hawaii a few days before. We shared and compared the horrors of that day. I saw Tony the day before his first marriage in Boston.

Folder D 11. Donna speaks about visiting Diane in South Dakota. The day we were to leave we could not find Wend's shoes. Wendi had hidden them in plain sight on a set of skis in the downstairs. Wendi was a handful even at age 3.

The Taylor high school class of 1963 was great at fundraising but never got around to completing the THS annual. The next year our class reformatted the pictures and had their annual printed. We then bought a trampoline for the high school and received permission to go on a skip trip. I believe this was a first skip trip in Taylor high school history. I believe I talked about it earlier. I am hoping to put together a 60th reunion for our class next year. I'm thinking of asking each to write a couple of pages about memories of this skip trip. I drove one car with two of my classmates in the front seat and two in the backseat where Frida Larson sat in the middle as chaperone for the car. Once again we rotated places at regular intervals. Mary Dohrmann joined our class to graduate early. Once as she was seated beside she grabbed the steering wheel as she felt I was inattentive to that curves in the road. I then took both hands off the steering wheel and soon she said you have to steer, you have to steer I said I won't touch the steering wheel until you let go of it which she finally did. The South Dakota legislature had change the drinking age from 3.2 % alcohol beer from 18 to 19. This law went into effect a week before we got to South Dakota so none of us could legally buy beer the entire trip.

March 6, 2015 I am, trying to prepare for my farm auction later this year. I'm taking my last truck load of wheat to South West Grain to sell. I finished combining winter wheat in December after the ground froze hard enough that I could drive a combine and pick up the swaths. I had pulled a combine out of the mud 13 times and the trucks perhaps an equal number. My legs are so weak I need both legs to operate the clutch on the truck and the brakes. I contemplate my retirement as being in a motorized wheelchair for the rest of my life. On April 4, 2023 I can walk well and do stairs fairly well.

Wendi is teaching physiology at the school where she learned massage therapy. She and Donna have been comparing notes about what it's like to have an active life growing inside you. I hear some of the joyful and woeful comments about kicking the abdomen and the spine and occasionally the bladder. My understanding of this joyful part of life is mostly academic. Not as a reality for those who have experienced it.

I told Donna that perhaps my headstone should read Arthur Hoyer Haugen Diers Dohrmann to acknowledge all my grandparents not just my father's last name. I thought my obit should be the trails to eternity. Starting from the house to the car the house to the barns, to the farm fields to Taylor and Fargo and beyond. The Ho Chi Minh Trail in Cambodia, hurricane Ridge in Washington state the Appalachian trail and the Gunflint Trail north of Duluth. This trail was one of the most beautiful in my memory. I hiked a high trail in the Swiss Alps to an

Army base where I spent the night. The longest and best trail was after meeting and marrying Donna. I'm returning from a five-week cruise around South America. What happens next I don't know.

Donna and I shared fascination with the Harry Potter series. We read and discussed each book as it appeared in order Donna would pre-order each book from B Dalton and we eagerly awaited the new arrival. Donna and I discussing the spiritual symbolism of some parts of this series. Because we read the books well in advance of seeing the movies I sometimes had difficulty reorientated myself to that particular timeline of the story. Some of Donna's pastor Associates felt that Harry Potter was pure heresy. We enjoyed the escape into fantasy. But we also spent a significant amount of time talking about analogies and allegories that we saw in the series. Donna discusses the theological implications of the Harry Potter series with her pastoral colleagues. I cannot restate her positions on what we read or observed but we were in very close agreement of the subjects we discussed. Other movies we watch together several times were the sound of music and fiddler on the roof. A very special time for us was to be in Austria where the sound of music was filmed. We also visited some of the sites in the Alps where the film was shot. It is much easier to discuss fictional events like the movies we shared that it was to talk about the real-life challenges. Nurturing children was so packed with our emotional preconceptions that getting a smile from her daughter would require hours of discussion. Our daughters and grandsons were the premier topics of discussion for as long as we had together. 47 years of shared experience allowed us to bounce from topic to topic often without any transitions. In most instances we knew what the other one was talking about although there were times it took a long time to get onto the same page.

Like the oak and Sycamore in the poem by Kai Gabran we did not grow too close together but our roots were intwined and we drew nourishment from the same soil. We enjoyed similar sun and rain and gentle breezes. We endured similar storms and darkness and fierce adversity. We laughed and cried at the same events. But when we laughed alone or cried alone we always had the opportunity to share our feelings. For us this was perfect. We spent a lot of time discussing our perceptions of other couples' relationships. Our first discussions were about how our parents related to one another and to their families. For my folks it seems like dad decided and mom followed. But they each made personal decisions that did not require the other person's input. Donna's folks seem to live entirely alone, being in the same house did not mean they were together. Perhaps the only time those folks were together is when their children were conceived. We found it almost incomprehensible that one person should sacrifice their individuality so that the other could succeed.

In our daily lives we would find that one would lead and the other would follow. The leadership was assigned to whoever knew most about the road we would travel. We also had many times when we struck out on her own and talked about events when we met again. We always believe it is important to meet again. Now I meet Donna only in my dreams! Day dreams of a wonderful but fading time, I am grateful that we tape recorded as much as we did. The DVD's of our earlier times are somewhere.

Road limitations three 1423

I found T-shirts at the end of the world yesterday but it did not have time to buy them todays tours were canceled. I was on a tour around South America when I wrote this.

Wintering cattle at elbow woods revised edition. As retold by Fred Dorman and Leland Brand and Fred Dohrmann. The cattle were moved north to Bailey's at Emerson where they were grazed until they had to be moved again. They may then move to the Hanson brothers place north of Marshall and then apparently move to Elbow woods for the winter. Dads version of this story did not include the brands cattle or the name where they held at Emerson. The Hanson boys operation was primarily run by their sister whose name I do not know. I remember seeing the Hanson boys driving Taylor Arnie Barney and unknown the three in the front seat of the car. One could drive one could see in one could hear but together they moved.

I remember seeing the picture of dad postmarked July 5 I believe 1933. He was standing in the middle of a muddy road in a black-and-white picture I told him it's black and white but his eyes were bloodshot. He said that he had gone to our for the Fourth of July powwow at Elbow woods and was just coming back at daylight when Kenneth took the picture of him. Until then I did not realize that too went to keep cattle they would spend summers putting up a and preparing the hay to feed the cattle. Apparently dad and whoever became Mrs. Joe Chase had a real thing going on. At Joe Chase's funeral dad Clarence and John attended John told me that dad and Mrs. Chase pretty much set by themselves the entire time until they had to leave. I know when we would go fishing dad would point out where all the people he had known had lived or currently live on the way to Lake Schakawa which covered the elbow woods townsite.

In 1934 they had to move the cattle home in mid-March as they had gotten moldy and was causing abortions and killing the cattle when they got the cattle to Marshall dad needed another horse which he bought from someone and it was poorly trained it balked and were reared and carried on dad stayed on it and the Hanson boys rolled on the ground laughing at him but he was afraid to get off of the horse so he rode the horse and stayed on the horse until he got to Taylor at which time he said he finally crawled off the horse and I have no idea what happened to the to the horse after that but dad laughed at the story when he told that if it wasn't laughing at the time he was experiencing it.

A story told by Lee brand about Dugan which was the name of Wilmer Dorman Kenneth Dohrmann's brother as he rode to school one day he saw a skunk. a skunk hide is worth a dollar so he jumped off the horse and killed a skunk with his history book needless to say he was not appreciated in school and I don't know that they ever were able to use the history book again but a dollar was were was a lot at that time. Apparently, the cattle that were lost on the trip to Taylor were skinned out by Dugan and Kenneth as that was the only salvage value they could get out of their livestock that died I don't know what the value was your what they did with the carcasses but one more way of preserving whatever value they could find

there were stockyards in Taylor Boyle and Gladstone that the railroad used to gather cattle and they would ship to Minneapolis or most likely Chicago. I remember seeing two large chests that Fred Dorman had bought in Chicago he bought material and other things for sewing clothes during the winter but hidden in the bottom were several pieces of candy for the kids I remember Florence and Carol talking about about opening the trunks expressing joy at the materials that they would could use to school clothing during the winter or at their spare time and a wonderful surprise of little bits of candy to show that their father truly love them. The owners of the cattle got free rise to Chicago and back they would have to unload the cattle apparently every hundred miles or so Sterling ND was the only site Dad talked about and I'm not certain what sites in Minnesota who unload the cattle feed them give him water and then load them back up for the sale in Chicago I believe the cattle were panned in the sales the buyers would come and inspect the cattle and make offers on each group. This was not at auction type that I was familiar with.

Another fall adventure that the Dohrmann families did they would take wagons with just just the reaches and would travel to the Badlands and cut cedar to be made into posts. dad described sitting on the 4 x 6 reaches on the way there but able to sit on the piles of logs that they brought. I'm certain some of the fencepost still on the ground were results of these trips I know Fred and Clarence retraced the route but I was not able to go with them so I'm not certain exactly where they cut the Cedar. Dad also talked about taking the truck too Camp Crook South Dakota where you would being back a load of the lodgepole pine. As I remember the poles were 24 feet long so they had to be tied down into the truck because a truck only had a 13 foot bed.

A story from apparently 2018 when I entered interviewed Leland Brand he was staying in Bismarck had Nancy's place going to another check up he has had incidences of hospitalization and always a concern but now in 2023 he's 101 years old as far as I know stilling living in the old stone hammer ranch being cared for by Dub (Barbra} Lynn and Nancy take turns to come back to live give double a break. At the time I complemented Leyland I said I studied his life as a father of girls watching now he and Gail were both welcoming and warning it was awkward because Lynn and Nancy were both there both of whom I have dated at various times. I felt at the time he needed to know how I felt about him there's no point in telling stories at a funeral you have to tell the people when they are alive.

An awkward story I told Leyland Nancy and Lynn is about one evening I was on a double date at the drive-in movie at intermission we went to the concession stand bought popcorn and drinks as we were discussing it we decided that we kind of like the other girl better than the one we were with so when we came back to the car we simply switched places I went from front seat to backseat and at the time I'm not certain if we asked the girls if that was a good deal or not Leland laughed and asked Nancy was that you and she said no not that she could remember but it was a story of the lighthearted fun we had as we were discussing the world and exploring life and just having fun.

On the way to the Badlands Bible camp 90th anniversary celebration I started a story I don't know if I finished but I have I have so many fond memories of the Badlands Bible They have a new site which I need to learn about Donna and I have been there and it is a beautiful site and well-financed many of the donors became oil millionaires and donated generously to the Badlands Bible. While in high school Clarence would fill a truck load of kids from the church in Taylor and we would ride to the Badlands Bible camp to clean it up and get it ready for occupation and cleaned in the mud to clean the dirt set up the bunks and had a wonderful time I'm certain now they would never allow 30 kids in open backend of a truck we had our sleeping bags we had some other supplies but it was a great event. There is this memory I have of the Badlands Bible camp was before the old site was even there the man slept upstairs in a barn and the women slept downstairs all I can remember is that the stone steps going up to the into the barn were so big they were almost to my waist so I apparently was quite small mom and dad said that yes we had been there when I was very little just learning to walk. Last summer they had a recognition event for those who donated for the Badlands Bible camp. I arrived looked around and went inside and talk to people that I had known had interesting conversations as the camp director Brent Seeks came to talk to each of the people of the table when they got to my table he said how did you get in here I thought I'll saw everybody who came in the door I said no I came in the back door I don't always come in the front door he laughed and said yeah I probably should've known that but it was an interesting time to talk to a lot of old people my age and reminisce and look forward to what the camp will be

September 5, 2018 I have worked at the farmstead to enclose the back entry way and to do some revision on a bike rack I want to put onto the RV as we prepare to head for to Florida. I stopped in Taylor bar for the coffee group who usually meets about 10 o'clock in the morning I have known about this but have never attended before I talk to Frank Zillich who is who was still working at the time and I saw him again just in January at James Marcusens and funeral. At the time I told Frank a Willieism {sayings Willie Severson used) how it now takes longer to rest than it does to get tired. We laughed and appreciated the knowledge that this information's said about an aging individual and group. Another Willieism about where are we we are always on this side of Chris Stoxen's place.

Sen. John McCain has died. The current president which I only referred to as 45 even though he is such a small bore has made more disparaging remarks about Sen. McCain. I did not agree with Sen. McCain but I always respected him. I cannot say that about 45 as even when he does things I approve of I cannot stand to acknowledge his existence as a human being.

September 8, 2018 Donna is driving as we go to Colorado. I remember other drives the one I'm talked about was there is a political meeting in Minot. I left Fargo after midnight as I turned off 94 to head north to Minot there was a female hitchhiker I stopped gave her a ride as we continued north I heard a bit of her story as we drove the sun came up I use my elbow to click in the tape player which played Here comes the Sun. I told Dona this woman is a template of her. As a junior in high school and a sociology class we learned that high achieving women left home early but come back much soonerthan men. I told Zane Paulson that this was the type of woman I would wait for. I am amazed I knew of Donna before I met her.

When we discussed our daughters we believed the mark of good teaching is when the student surpasses the instructor. We are always amazed that our grandsons have an opportunity to excel in an environment we cannot imagine. Plato taught that humans could only see shadows of reality. Aristotle the student taught a more comprehensible vision of reality. Unfortunately the leaders of his society did not want to hear what he talked. So he drank hemlock what we now believe is similar to drinking the Kool-Aid. We do not believe in going quietly into that good night. We will fight for the right to speak truth to those in power.

The first night Donna and I slept together we did that. We arrived at the old farmhouse late at night my folks were in Alaska Maryanne was not there to chaperone. As we were undressing I realize I stank. No showers in the old farmhouse so they went upstairs took a bath by the time it was done we were to. Sex is too important to be anything but friendly fun and fantastic. We slept that night and thoroughly enjoyed the morning.

Wondering since March 2018 we took the new RV to California near LA we visited Garrett the North to San Francisco. The best week was at Pismo beach as the weather was wonderful and beaches were beautiful. We continued north hoping to see Portland and Seattle. But the weather was cool and rainy. One evening Donna said let's go home. By morning I told her change the reservations plan a trip and I will drive us there. We drove to Boise and onto Cheyenne where we left her motorhome in the went to visit Wendi. The next summer we headed east through Minneapolis Rochester Minnesota where we visited Derek and onto Lily Lake were we visited Gene and Peggy Redlin. On through Indianapolis Indiana my least favorite town in the world to drive through. The last two times were in the rain with five lanes of semi's and road construction so we could not see when the lanes shifted. I just tried to stay between the trucks. At this time Donna went into the bedroom in the back read a book and came out when the traffic cleared. We visited Cincinnati for a surprise birthday party for Diane. The party her daughters had planned for her was a true surprise. We were told not to arrive at the country club until after 7 PM. Diane always there early bird called us twice and finally walked down to the carriage house where we were staying to try to marches off to get there early. Donna said with a twisted grin that was the only time she had thwarted Diane's demands.

Scary Roads

The farmhouse and our family grew over the years. The original mail order house had a kitchen, dining room, living room and bedroom on the main floor. Up stairs was a bedroom and bathroom. Two entryways, two upstairs bedrooms, and an expanded living room and bedroom were added on the main floor. As mom had more children a hierarchy of rooms were established. The first two or three years were in a room off the dining room in the old farmhouse. Naomi was the first to stay alone in her room upstairs. A couple years later I joined her and we slept in the same bed for perhaps two years. Since I didn't want to wake up right away in the morning when dad called up the stairs Naomi would nicely pour part of about a glass of water on me to wake me up. I think that happen once after that I fainted sleep and as she came in the room with a glass of water I would hit it and splash it on her. Dennis finally graduated to an upstairs bedroom which we shared together and Naomi was back on her own. Dennis was not happy about being upstairs and one night I told him a scary story. It was so bad he began to cry and ran down the steps into the kitchen where mom and dad attempted to console him. Dennis was so upset he threw up on the kitchen floor. Dad came up the steps lifted me out of bed in my pajamas carried me downstairs and use me to wipe up the kitchen floor. Made a mess my pajamas and he said take them off clean the floor wash it and never tell that kind of stories again. I think I learned in one lesson. There are three bedrooms upstairs and the farmhouse when I joined. A hired man and a hired girl slept in different rooms upstairs. When Dennis joined the upstairs gang an old chicken coop was converted outside and I hired man slept there. Lucille joined Naomi in her bedroom and then when it came time for Russell to come upstairs the three boys slept in one room. When Priscilla was old enough to move upstairs she and Lucille move into the room that the hired girl had occupied. Naomi took over pretty much full-time as first assistant childcare provider. Erna finally joined the upstairs gang with Lucille Priscilla and herself. Dad gleefully took over the nursery as an office. This room we would enter if the door was open but if the door was closed it had better be an emergency before you knocked on the door and disturbs dads bookkeeping.

I believe it was about 1952 when we got our first television set. The entire family would sit on the couch on the floor and dad in his recliner. We generally had a choice of two stations from Bismarck. Then dad bought power rotating antenna and we were able to get a station from Monot. Years later I tease dad that once they had TV they had no more children. Mom's first child was stillborn. Naomi was born and then Armin who lived only a few days. A family of seven children was about average for the community at that time. The largest family I know had 12 children. Other than Loran Myran I didn't know of any single child families. Dad had O negative blood type. This was a universal donor blood. Loren's life was saved because dad rushed to the hospital to donate blood to give him a transfusion which allowed him to live. Loren older sibling did not survive because of lack of blood transfusion. After we got the rural telephone is not unusual to get a call for dad to rush to Dickinson to give blood for transfusion. I once asked how many lives he had saved but he professed not to know or remember. Now I cannot remember the blood disorder that cause children to die soon after birth.

The first electricity we had in the house that I can vaguely remember was 32 V direct current. We had a 60 foot wind tower on the farmstead was later became one of my favorite hiding spots. There is a gasoline powered generator in the pumphouse whether first wells were located. This we also had a large selection of batteries for the times when the wind didn't blow we could last a couple of hours without having to start the generator. I believe the house had a propane stove and water heater. The heat was provided by a coal furnace downstairs. This was her gravity flow system with large ductwork running throughout the house. Rural electric power brought many great changes to life on the farm. The one I like most was in electric stoker to feed the furnace and fans to move the heat around the house. The coal stoker allowed heat all night. No longer did you have to go down twice a night to shovel it in more coal shaker grates to get the fire burning and take ashes out of the stove. Tending the stoker in carrying out the ashes soon became my job. The basement was a dirty place we dumped coal into the basement to her coal chute we would attempt to get enough to last through the winter. moving the ashes meant dust was prevailing. The canning room was the other major portion of the basement. The walls were lined with shelves so that in the fall of the year the produce of the large garden that our family tended were stored also beef and pork that was butchered was canned and stored in the basement my favorite part was a 50 gallon crock of sauerkraut that had a place in the canning room. Each time I was sent down to get something for a meal I would move the cover and reach in and get a finger full of sauerkraut still my favorite memory. Mom would send us down to fetch something but the descriptions were tough she finally wrote North South East and West on the walls so that we had our reference to where to look for what she wanted. I have read many stories about how a woman's nutrition when she was pregnant affected her children and grandchildren. This probably needs more study than trying to figure out why somebodies index finger is longer than their ring finger or why they have blue eyes or brown eyes.

I believe it is about 1960 after dad had been elected as director for West Plains cooperative that the house was changed to all electric. Holes were drilled in the outside wall of the house and insulation was blown in to fill the spaces. The exterior was then covered with a thin Styrofoam insulation and all steel siding. This siding is still on the house and looks to be in very good shape. The house had been built from a kit I believe ordered from Sears and Roebuck in 1940. The interior walls were basically I pressed cardboard. I don't know that there was even insulation between the boards on the outside and the wood siding added later. The original house had a front porch mudroom added first. Then a two-story addition was added which extended the living room added the nursery or dad's office and two upstairs bedrooms. I don't know when the upstairs bathroom was put there but I do remember an outhouse for the first years of my life. The first baths I remember where in a large laundry sink in the porch.

The water from our wells was awful. It was high in alkali and extremely hard. You needed to acclimate your system to the water or else a glass of water would completely flush your system. We never needed laxatives as long as we live there. Grandfather Fred first attempted to live about a half mile northwest of the farmstead. Grandma Louise said the water was so bad that they had to move. A number of wells were dug until they found the water at what they called the snow village ranch. This water was soft but very high in sodium. Eventually Clarence dug a well over 10,000 feet down to find better water. This water was high sodium but could be conditioned for drinking purposes. Dad dug several before he found one marginally acceptable. This water was softened for household and laundry use. Eventualy we acclimated to drink it. After I bought the farm house from Russell a year and a half before he died I had to replace all the plumbing in the house. The cast iron drains were completely rotted away all the metal pipes were corroded so that hardly let water flow. The Southwest water pipeline was probably a better addition to the house and electricity. Russ and Cindy lived with the fact it took 15 min. to draw a tub of water to take a bath. I remodel the bathroom by adding a shower moving the stool and the wall to the room. I took the metal roof off the hog barn that was falling down. I burn the barn and used to steel roofingto fix up the north side of the garage. When Russell was raising hogs they dug the foundation out from the hog barn the large barn and the garage. The first thing I did was put the buildings back on the foundations. I'm still working on the old barn. All the outbuildings at the firm said had new steel put on their roof and steel siding on the sides it finally looks like something besides a dump ground. I am much happier designing, building or even repairing things that do not run away.

The farm house we bought from Dennis and Barbara was all electric heat but had about 2 feet of uninsulated plywood in the basement. I insulated the basement and added a coal furnace to that house. The cost of heating that house was less than half after coal furnace was installed. Dennis and Russell enjoyed working with cattle much more than dealing with anything mechanical. Russell's happiest years were when he was an insurance agent at the bank and rented the farmland to me. He kept the cattle until he died. Dennis has sold or rented all his farmland and is struggling to take care of the cattle that he is turned over to Cory. Dennis's health is precarious I don't believe he will ever have a retirement.

About 10 years ago I started planting trees at the old farmstead. The shelter belt dad planted in the 1940s has pretty well reached the end of its lifespan. The new trees protect the old farmstead and mark out a 6 acre site where another house can be built. I'm bringing water into that site this spring. The trees planted around the site I call a Memorial Grove. My original thought was Lyle I connot remember his last name" I guy I called super Republican because he always had an elephant on his lapel. We discussed politics so much nobody wanted to sit at the same table with us after church. I learned to treasure someone with whom I could disagree with and we never became disagreeable. We both admitted to changing some of our beliefs because of what we learned from the other. Since then Roger Palmer, Ken Bergo, Keith and Ginny Dehnert and Donna Dohrmann had joined the ever-growing list of people I remember as a work on the trees. Perhaps someday I will put up a plaque.

Every time I approach the farmstead I see or think of things that need to be done. This is a never-ending project but I am happy to know that it's better now than when I started. After a year and half wondering I know that I have to move ahead even if the direction I goal is a dead end I need to find forward. This chapter went nowhere that I originally had intended.

I had my car rigged up with two switches one would ground out the coil and cause the car to stall and quit. The other one gave a shock to the far right of the passenger seat. One evening I drove Priscilla and Carol Hutchison to a movie in Dickinson. On the way home I started the story of the Man with the Golden arm. As the story progressed, I flicked the switch and a car would hesitate and it will and stop and go as

I got to the darkest spot almost a half-mile from the farmstead I turned it off and the car quit I tried turning the key and nothing happened I told them I would walk to the farmstead and get another car as I opened the door they both screamed and said no! I said sometimes the car would start after it cooled down and I roll down the window because it was a warm night. They both objected they wanted the windows tight and doors locked. I asked if they wanted to hear the rest of the story. No. Eventually I started the car and drove them back. The shock wire was never used. I removed the modifications before I went to college with another car.

All my life I have found that I see better in low light situations than most anyone else around me. The first instance was as I was about 6th grade. Several of were running around Taylor after dark as we ran behind a house everyone else tripped over a low fence. None of them had seen the fence and could not believe I had. In Vietnam I could move easily at night without a flashlight as I had no intention of letting anyone know of my presence. Donna accused me of being part bird and part cat, to cheep to use a flashlight because I could see in the dark.

Sunrise Roads

March 11, 2015 I walked the farmstead before sunrise look around and try to remember the good and say goodbye to what we be sold next month. Dennis and Cory will be coming out to help me later this morning I think about the many sunrises I have seen at this farmstead. In my high school years I would usually feed cattle first thing in the morning. The weather would be 10,20,30 or more below zero when I start the tractor in the shed let it warm little bit open the doors and begin the day. I get the load of hay drive to the gate and open it up as I move to the area where I feed the cows I can hear them as they get up and move. In this cold weather I even hear there hides crack as a get up and move is the ice that is formed on them breaks amble out to where I have spent the first second and third load of a about this time the sun would come up. There are friends in high school who said they haven't seen the sun for the a month and I say I see it just about every morning it seems like it sunrise there is a narrow crack in the eastern horizon between the low hills and the low clouds and I see the sun as it appears in this crack for a few minutes to half an hour and then is gone behind the clouds for the rest of the day.

The next chore was to milk the cows. We would bring them in from the corral give him a little bit to eat before milking, for about two years we had milk by hand we usually milk between three and five cows each day. The last two years we bought a milking machine which speeded the process up and allowed us to do other chores while the cows are being milked. Some operations would have a time in the summer when they didn't milk but the family always had a need for milk and cheese and butter so we milked the year around. The cream that was not used for the family we sold as a cash income another income source was the excess milk that we produced we then bought hogs to feed them out to and get another income source. Hogs require a lot of attention and work. I remember one morning mom came rushing into the house all on a breath she had looked out the window and seeing hogs in her garden she proceeded to a stampede them out the garden and it's our job to find him and bring him back and try to get them into the pens. I think the only thing that would stop the hogs was woven wire fence dug 3 feet into the ground and 6 feet into the air. But we didn't have that chance so we constantly battled to contain the hogs. I remember one day when the little pigs are about five or 6 pounds I brought one into show to Donna I thought it was cute, she took one look at it and said it's just a pig take it away. Farrowing guilts took a special touch. You needed to feed them correctly so they gain weight but didn't get fat. The hour or so it took for pigs to be born was a long boring time. After about 20 min. if they were not done giving birth I gave them a shot of OxyContin a smooth muscle stimulant and then wait some more usually as soon as the baby page were born we would catch them and clip their needle teeth so that when they nurse they did not cut the mothers nipples. And about a week we would castrate the boars and then it was a waiting game until they weaned and fed him up to butcher.

I'm watching a hawk as it flies above the farmstead and I think of the hours I have spent watching hawks hunt as I am driving the tractor, they a circle around to get gophers. Their favorite is the baby rabbits that are flushed out by the fieldwork. One day I watched to hawks hunting on a hillside, the hawks would come swooping down but very often immediately took off of this was unusual, Normally when they caught their prey they would stay on the ground until they had it killed as I got closer I noticed something else moving in the tall grass here were two coyotes walking around trying to catch mice and the hawks were watching as apparently if the mouse was more than 10 feet from the coyote the hawk would strike at it and of course the coyote immediately then attacked in an attempt to get the mouse. I think this was the first time I had seen the two hunters working the same area.

In my early years of farming when I did summer falllow I would often flush out I hen pheasant with the baby chicks. she had to run across open ground to where they could find cover again. In one instance I watched as a hawk dived for the chicks that hen pheasant jumped into the air and hit the hawk both birds recovered and the hawk flew up to attempt to attack again I believe at least three times that I saw the hen pheasant interrupt the hawks attack. I always cheered for the pheasants not so much for the rabbits the gophers and the mice. Early once spring I saw a golden eagle in the field and it looked like it was eating on something suddenly the eagle flew up and as I watched an antelope doe came running at where the eagle had been I didn't know until several hours later that I could see that apparently the that antelope fawn had died and the eagle was trying to provide food for its young and a half hour or so that antelope would wander off the eagle would return for another. an attempt to lift it off. The eagle could drag it about 20 or 30 feet at which time the doe would come running at it again. I knew eventually the eagle would get its prey and was early enough that doe could probably rebreed and have another fawn that year.

June 12 I'm on my way to Sioux Falls South Dakota to Lonnie and Cher Lynn's wedding. In the last couple of months I have had a taste of retirement. Donna states that retirement is working better for me than for her. The wind farm proposal for our area of Stark County has been defeated and moved to Hettinger County. There are too many people who did not want to see a windmill. For me the loss of $30,000 a year for 30 years is a big hole to fill. Our family Christmas party could be interesting this year. Dennis and Barb are scheduled to host it but I fear the break between Ron and Dennis is permanent. Dennis's financial loss is greater than mine and as I record this in 2023 that split is still not even close to being repaired.

A random recollection one Sunday morning in winter when we were living in Fargo Arlie and I decided to go on a drive about to Red Lake Falls and just look at different parts of the Valley. As we were wondering North I looked down and realized that I was nearly out of fuel. We were approaching a small town in Minnesota and we stopped about a quarter-mile out of town tucked the top down on my convertible Fiat and drove into town at nine o'clock in the morning there is not a lot of activity that we eventually saw a church that people were leaving so we stopped and asked if there is any access to gasoline typical small town everybody knew who to call to so they made a phone call and the individual came down to the gas station is expressly on Sunday morning to give us enough gas to be on her way. After filling gas and not being absolute idiots we put the car top back up and continued our drive. Another Sunday morning I came home to THE PAD(tenement house encouraging perversion and debauchery) about five o'clock in the morning and a bunch of people were going to go skiing being up for anything I agreed and we headed off I believe they slept the entire way. About 330 that afternoon as I was going up the T-bar I was with another individual who asked if I was having fun I said yes but the it's getting dark and I'm having trouble seeing some of the moguls as I go down the hill. He asked how long I had been skiing I said well we got there about 10 o'clock said to have you taken a break? no have you had anything to eat I said well I had two hard-boiled eggs in my pocket I didn't tell him I had a half pint of whiskey also. He gave me his sternness look and said when you get down to the bottom of the hill quick you're just an accident waiting to happen I took his advice and eventually returned back to Fargo having another wonderful day of memories.

Printed in the United States
by Baker & Taylor Publisher Services